Harvey Davis &

A Most Important Collection of High Art Objects from China

and Japan

Property of M. Sichel, rue Pigalle, Paris, and R.A. Robertson, Yokohama,

Japan

Harvey Davis &

A Most Important Collection of High Art Objects from China and Japan
Property of M. Sichel, rue Pigalle, Paris, and R.A. Robertson, Yokohama, Japan

ISBN/EAN: 9783337175474

Printed in Europe, USA, Canada, Australia, Japan

Cover: Foto ©Thomas Meinert / pixelio.de

More available books at **www.hansebooks.com**

NOW ON FREE EXHIBITION

AT THE

GALLERY OF THE PHILADELPHIA SOCIETY OF ARTISTS,

No. 1725 CHESTNUT STREET.

A MOST IMPORTANT COLLECTION

OF

HIGH ART OBJECTS

FROM

CHINA AND JAPAN.

PROPERTY OF

M. SICHEL, RUE PIGALLE, PARIS,

AND

R. A. ROBERTSON, YOKOHAMA, JAPAN.

The Whole to be Sold at Auction, Positively Without Reserve,

ON

MONDAY, TUESDAY AND WEDNESDAY AFTERNOONS,

MAY 22d, 23d and 24th,

At 3 O'Clock Prompt each day,

AT THE ABOVE GALLERY.

Mr. Thos. E. Kirby, of New York, has been engaged to conduct the sale.

MESSRS. DAVIS & HARVEY, AUCTIONEERS.
1882.

Note.

*The undersigned call particular attention to the arti-
cles described in this Catalogue—objects far superior
to those usually disposed of at auction. Mr. Richard
Austin Robertson, a resident of Japan and China for
the past nine years, contributes a collection of rareties
of an exceptional standard and impossible to dupli-
cate. M. Sichel, whose establishment, No. 11 Rue
Pigalle, Paris, is familiar to all our connoisseurs, contributes principally the Antique Chinese Porcelains
and solid color specimens, all of which are of exceedingly fine quality.*

*The specimens of Japanese Metal Work, including
Magnificent Bronzes, Daimio Swords, and Cabinet
Specimens, are remarkably fine and of marvelous
workmanship. The superb lacquers are the perfection
of Art, and like the Ivory Carvings, Japanese Ceram-
ics, Rich Stuffs (Mandarin and Daimio Robes, etc.),
Curios, etc., are of a quality sought by connoisseurs
and collectors, and should command more than ordinary notice.*

*A large collection of Kake-monos (Japanese Hang-
ing Scrolls) is included, among which are many examples, by Japan's Greatest Ancient and Modern Mas-
ters.*

*In fact the Sichel-Robertson Collection is an extra-
ordinary one. Never before have we had the pleasure of
offering to the public of Philadelphia so many desir-
able High Class Objects.*

*At the request of the owners, we have engaged Mr.
Thos. E. Kirby of New York to conduct the sale.*

Respectfully,

DAVIS & HARVEY.

CONDITIONS OF SALE.

1. The highest Bidder to be the Buyer, and if any disputes arise between two or more Bidders, the Lot so in dispute shall be immediately put up again and re-sold.

2. The Purchasers to give their names and addresses, and to pay down twenty-five per cent. on the dollar in part payment, or the whole of the Purchase-money, *if required*, in default of which the Lot or Lots so purchased to be immediately put up again and re-sold.

3. The Lots to be taken away at the Buyer's Expense and Risk at the conclusion of the Sale, and the remainder of the Purchase-money to be absolutely paid, or otherwise settled for to the satisfaction of the Vendors, on or before delivery : in default of which the Auctioneers will not hold themselves responsible, if the Lots be lost, stolen, damaged, or destroyed, but they will be left at the sole risk of the Purchaser.

4. The Sale of any Painting, Engraving, Print, piece of Furniture, Work of Art, or any other article, is not to be set aside on account of any error in the description. All articles are exposed for Public Exhibition one or more days, and are sold just as they are without recourse.

5. To prevent inaccuracy of delivery, no Lot can, on any account, be removed without presentation of the bill.

6. Failing to comply with the above conditions, the money deposited in part payment shall be forfeited.

DAVIS & HARVEY.

Notice.

It was our intention to have held this sale in February last, but owing to the non-arrival of goods, and being unable to get possession of the gallery of the Philadelphia Society of Artists at an earlier date, we have been compelled to make the sale at the present late season when many of our customers have left the city. We regret this fact, but under the circumstances cannot do otherwise than carry out the wishes of owners and make the sale at the present time.

According to instructions, the sale will be a positive one ; every lot will be sold to the highest bidder.

DAVIS & HARVEY.
THOS. E. KIRBY.

CATALOGUE.

First Day's Sale.

1 Japanese porcelain small Plates.　　　3 pieces
2 Antique pottery Turtle.
3 Two small perfume Boxes *bleu de Nankin* and crackle ware.　　　2 pieces
4 Odd shape Trays, Japanese manufacture.

　　　3 pieces
5 Raku and Kioto ware small Cups.　　　2 pieces
6 Antique araku Tea Jar, relief ornamentation and metal top.
7 Old Chinese Pottery, bowl lotus form, splash glaze inside and out.
8 Chinese rosedon Bowl, *pear d'u orange* surface (slightly defective.)

9 Pair small Japanese bronze Vases, finely wrought.
2 pieces

10 Turquoise leaf shape Tray, old Kishiu ware.

11 Antique Japanese pottery Perfume Boxes.
2 pieces

12 Araku Trays, gray glaze with ornamentation in white.
2 pieces

13 Japanese short Sword, fine blade. .

14 Very fine porcelain small Plates, royal Imari and egg shell.
2 pieces

15 Choice turquoise Vase, delicately crackled beneath glaze, Japanese manufacture.

16 Small Saki Cups, various makes, Chinese and Japanese.
4 pieces

17 Porcelain Cups and small Vases, assorted specimens.
5 pieces

18 Ancient Chinese bronze Incense Burner, engraved ornamentation and mark of the Ming period, has teak wood stand.

19 Handsome royal Hezin porcelain Bowl, decoration of fishes, water, etc., on *rouge corail* ground.

20 Antique Kioto Rice Jar, richly decorated in green and blue enamels and gold.

21 Fine antique Kishiu Dish, lotus design, engraved ornamentation beneath turquoise glaze.

22 Chinese brown crackle Bottle, blue decorati on.

23 Japanese blue and white Plate.

24 Chinese porcelain Pitcher, antique shape, enameled floral decoration.

25 Old Hammered bronze Incense Burner.

26 Choice modern Satsuma Bowl, finely decorated, figure of priest inside, maple leaves outside.

27 Fine porcelain Bottle, olive green glaze, metalic lustre.

28 Japanese pottery Incense Jar, veins of marble effect—rare specimen.

29 Exquisitely decorated antique Kioto Bowl.

30 Very fine antique Kutani Fruit Stand, decoration in rich colors.

31 Handsome awata ware Water Bottle, decoration of insects, etc., in choice colors.

32 Fine Japanese porcelain blue and white Teapots. 2 pieces

33 ——— Others, different. 2 pieces

34 Richly decorated antique Imari porcelain saki Bottle.

35 Old copper Plate, enameled and lacquered ornamentation.

36 Banko Yaki scroll shape Tray, exquisite ornamentation of flying stork, etc.

37 Pair carved soapstone Figures, Chinese. 2 pieces

38 Chinese porcelain Teapot, mottled green glaze.

39 Old Japanese porcelain Cups and Saucers. 3 pieces

40 Araku Trays, grey glaze decoration in white reserve. 2 pieces

41 Elegant modern Satsuma Incense Burner, decorated with figures of deities, etc., lotus flower in relief on cover.

42 Chinese crackle ware Vase, ovoid form, sea green glaze, with figures, etc., in brilliant colors.

43 Handsome *Blue de Nankin* Jar, symbolical and cloud design in deep blue, Kang-he period (slightly defective).

44 Ancient cream Jar and Cover, enameled ornamentation, grotesque figures of frogs, octopus, fish, etc.

45 Chinese *Vert de Mer* Incense Burner figure of Dog Foo.

46 Fine modern Satsuma Bowl, exquisitely decorated with diaper pattern, flowers, etc.

47 Ancient Japanese porcelain fish-shape Vase.

48 Very fine old Chinese gold bronze Fire Bowl, Ming period.

49 Elegantly modeled Satsuma Group—birds, flowers, etc.

50 Large and fine Owari porcelain Hibachi and Cover, choice blue decoration beneath glaze.

51 Superb lacquered Glove Box, ornamentation in pure gold and pearl.

52 Fine Nagasaki porcelain Vase interesting decoration of fishes swimming, etc.

53 Antique Bizen fire Bowl, brown splash glaze, and relief ornamentation of dragons, fire ball, etc.

54 Old Chinese sea-green China Plates, enameled ornamentation of flowers and insects, blue seal mark.   2 pieces

55 Fine old Satsuma Bowl, decoration of flowers in bright colors inside and outside.

56 —— Another, fantastic animals inside, maple leaves outside.

57 Choice Japanese egg-shell Cups, Saucers, and Covers, decorated with figures on brilliant red ground.   2 pieces

58 Small coupe, antique Chinese porcelain *sang de Boeuf*, glaze, Kang-he period.

59 Very fine Chinese crackle ware Pih-tung, rich green glaze.

60 Elegant cloisonne enamel Plaque, rich design of birds, etc., on salmon color ground, finest quality of modern work.   Diameter 12 inches.

61 Beautiful royal kaga Bowl, square form, decoration in precious metal on crimson ground, deep blue inside.

62 Fine old Chinese Bottle, Kang-he period, *Gros Bleu* glaze, with slight decoration in gold.

63 Very fine old Chinese Plate, decoration in brilliant colors, Chinese domestic scene, etc.

64 Old Chinese pottery Basket, *gris-perle* crackle glaze.

65 Handsomely lacquered Work-box, with compartments inside.

66 Carved alabaster Chinese Shrine.

67 Very fine modern Satsuma Teapot, exquisitely decorated with gold and delicate colors.

68 Fine Nagasaki porcelain Bureau Set, handsomely decorated.   4 pieces

69 Rare and fine old Chinese porcelain Bowl, turquoise glaze inside and outside.

70 Antique kioto Bowl, finely decorated with figures of Japanese poets and painters, in choice colors.

71 Royal Imari porcelain Trays, octagonal forms, brilliant decorations.   2 pieces

72 Fine Chinese *flambé* Vase.

73 Elegant old Chinese porcelain Bowl, decoration of fruit, flowers, leaves, etc., Kea-king period.

74 Rare and fine " grains of rice " Plate, decoration in fine blue beneath glaze, Yung-ching period.

75 Ancient Japanese iron Vase, medallions exquisitely inlaid with gold and silver.

76 Superb black and gold lacquer Card-box, with four small boxes inside, a choice specimen of the finest quality of modern lacquer.

77 Finely decorated Satsuma Fire Bowl, Japanese historical scenes in medallions.

78 Handsome *Bleu de Nankin* Vase, decorated with Chinese hunting scenes, fine specimen of Kang-he period ; has teak wood stand. Height and diameter 15x6 inches.

79 Exceedingly fine and rare Chinese Bowl, white engraved ground with exquisitely painted figures, green glaze inside, Këen-lung period (slightly broken, repaired).

80 Fine old Rosedon Saucer.

81 Chinese *pate tendre* small Vase, engraved ornamentation.

82 Very fine Chinese bronze Incense Burner, choice form and color, antique specimen.

83 Rare old Ming Bottle, crimson splash glaze.

84 Imperial yellow Saucers, engraved decoration of five-claw dragons in green, Kang-he period. 2 pieces

85 Japanese short Sword.

86 Choice Satsuma Bowl, exquisite and exceedingly fine ornamentation in gold, embossed work and colors.

87 —— Another, equally as fine, decorated on inside only.

88 Superb black lacquer Tray on feet, most exquisite ornamentation in pure gold and pearl, fan designs, highest class of modern lacquer.

89 —— Another, smaller.

90 Fine Kiyoto porcelain fan shape Box and Cover, Tokio decoration.

91 Antique Japanese crackle Tray, relief ornamentation of Devil fish and frogs.

92 Richly decorated Imari porcelain Bowl.

93 Splendid turquoise Bottle, crackle beneath glaze.

94 Very fine old *bleu de Nankin* Plaque, dragons, flowers, etc., in rich blue beneath glaze.

95 Rare and fine antique Chinese Coupe, rich rosedon splash glaze.

96 Corean pottery Bowl, repaired with gold cement.

97 Curious antique Chinese Figure, sacred beast, mottled green glaze, finely carved teak-wood stand.

98 Fine Kaga Bowl, rich crimson and gold decoration.

99 Elegant old Chinese turquoise Beaker, fine quality of Kang-he period (slightly defective).

100 Pair handsome Chinese Vases, flat bottle shape, finely decorated with figures, flowers, etc., in brilliant colors, pink enameled sides.   2 pieces

101 Exceedingly fine Satsuma Bowl, exquisitely decorated.

102 —— Another, smaller, decorated with figure of Japanese children playing.

103 Small *bleu de Nankin* Bottle, choice in color, 6 marks.

104 Handsome Pekin enamel Tête-á-tête set, comprising teapot, sugar-bowl, creamer, two cups and saucers and tray.

105 Splendid Kioto porcelain Tea Jar, exquisitely decorated in fine colors and gold, Japanese children's holiday procession.

106 Rare and curious Japanese crackle ware large Bowl, celadon glaze, enameled and painted, decoration, octopus, fish, etc.

107 Handsome old *bleu de Nankin* Vase, straight form, with flaring top, decoration of equestrian figure, etc. beneath glaze, height 18 inches.

108 Richly decorated Kaga Bowl, figure and flowers in medallion.

109 Rare and fine old Chinese Vase, *foi de veau* glaze, Kang-he period.

110 Set exquisitely lacquered Tray and four Card Boxes, finest quality.

111 Finely crackled Satsuma Bottle, enameled ornamentation, of grotesque figure, frogs at combat.

112 Fine modern Nankin Vase, jar shape, brilliant decoration, Chinese domestic scenes, height and diameter 15 x 6 inches.

113 Beautiful antique Chinese porcelain Bowl and Cover, fine quality of rosedon glaze ; rare and exceedingly fine specimen.

114 Fine modern Satsuma Bowl, handsome decoration inside and out, Daimio figures, etc.

115 Choice Chinese porcelain Bottle, *Bleu de Roi* glaze, engraved ornamentation.

116 Exquisitely decorated Kaga Saki Cup.

117 Pair very fine Nebishima porcelain Bowls, fine decoration in gold, crests, etc., in green medallions.

2 pieces

118 Elegant Chinese *Blanc de chine* Vase, engraved ornamentation beneath glaze, Kang-he period.

119 Superb modern lacquer Tray, oval form on feet, ornamentation in pure gold on black ground, highest grade.

120 Modern Nankin Vase, raised ornaments, blue and gold decoration. Height and diameter 12x6 inches.

121 Fine little Teapot. form of pomegranate, stem forming handle, exquisite decoration.

122 Very rare and fine antique Chinese Bowl, Këen-lung period, green glaze with metallic lustre, engraved ornamentation beneath, of imperial dragon.

123 Handsome antique Chinese porcelain Fruit Stand, enameled decoration of flowers, etc., flying bats, and crest inside in *rouge coraill*.

124 Ancient Chinese bronze Beaker, showing peculiar effects of age, Ming period, has teakwood stand.

125 Large and valuable antique Chinese Beaker, *Bleu poudre* glaze. Height and diameter 19x14 inches.

126 Superb Chinese ivory white fire Bowl, with finely carved teakwood stand and cover.

127 Choice liver color Saucer, very even glaze.

128 Exquisitely decorated Satsuma Bowl, design of chrysanthemum flowers, etc., in delicate colors and gold.

129 —— Another, smaller and older, delicately crackled, figure of priest, etc., outside, crest inside.

130 Handsome royal Imari Tray, finely decorated with figures, crests, etc., in choice colors.

131 Very fine antique Chinese celadon Vase, bottle shape, with ring handles. Height and diameter 12x4 inches.

132 Richly decorated Kaga Bowl.

133 Small Vase, old Chinese, *soufflé*, double diamond shape, teakwood stand.

134 Valuable Chinese ancient bronze hanging Vase, flat bottle form. showing very rich effects of color from age, Ming dynasty, 12x10 inches, has silk bag.

135 Very fine antique Kioto Teapot, ornamented in relief with dragons.

136 Choice Chinese Vase, lemon yellow glaze, decoration of figures of priests, pine tree, etc. Height and diameter 12x4 inches.

137 Old Ming porcelain Screen, decoration of figures, landscape scenery, etc., teakwood stand.

138 Antique Kioto Saki Bottle, beautifully crackled, handsomely enameled decoration of crests, etc.

139 Handsomely decorated Nagasaki Bureau Set, pair bottles and powder boxes.

140 Handsome old *Bleu de Nankin* Vase, biberon form, decoration of flying birds, flowers, etc., Kang-he period. Height 10 inches.

141 Pair richly decorated royal Imari Trays, octagonal form. 2 pieces

142 Handsome Chinese porcelain Bowl, octagonal form, finely decorated in blue and colors, figures of children playing, in white reserve.

143 Beautifully lacquered, Daimio lady's Cabinet, with three drawers and two compartments.

144 Japanese crackle ware Saki Bottle, double gourd shape, celadon glaze, with enameled decorations of octopus, fish, turtle, toads, etc.

145 Splendid ancient Chinese bronze Vase, very rich in color, engraved band top and bottom, scroll handles. Height and diameter 17x8 inches, an exceedingly fine and valuable specimen.

146 Fine old Satsuma Bowl, decoration of chrysanthemum flowers in medallions.

147 Superb Tokio Tea Jar, decorated with figure of priest, boy and tiger, etc.

148 Handsome black lacquer Card Set, tray and two boxes, all exquisitely ornamented with pure gold, finest grade of modern lacquer.

149 Beautiful Chinese rosedon Vase, biberon form, decoration over the glaze of cherry tree in blossom, etc. Height and diameter 12x7. Kang-he period ; a very choice specimen.

150 Exceedingly fine old *bleu de Nankin* Beaker, decoration of religious emblems, vases, ornaments, etc. Height and diameter 17x7 inches, ring and flower mark.

151 —— Another, different shape, decoration in dark blue of figure, etc., ring mark of the Kang-he period. Height and diameter 17x8 inches.

152 Small Satsuma bottle-shape Vase, delicately crackled and exquisitely decorated in embossed gold and enamels.

153 Fine old Chinese Këen-lung Bowl, engraved apple-green glaze, with floral ornamentation.

154 Very old and fine Chinese gold bronze cylindrical Vase, with teakwood stand, Ming period.

155 Set exquisite small Trays, finest quality of lacquer, with gold decoration and pearl inlaid.   3 pieces

156 Fine *bleu de Nankin* Plate, "grains of rice " border.

157 Rare old Chinese imperial yellow Vase, engraved decoration of Dog-Foo in colors. Height and diameter 12x6 inches.

158 Pair very fine Tokio Vases, handsomely decorated in choice colors, Japanese, domestic, and historical scenes. Height and diameter 12x4 inches.
                                                    2 pieces

159 Handsome pearl Tray, shape of fish, finely carved.

160 Valuable antique Chinese gold bronze Bowl, hexagonal form, with scolloped edge, engraved ornamentation, Ming period.

161 Magnificent black and gold lacquer impeiial Writing Case, furnished with ink-stone and bronze water bottle, crests and blossoms in pure gold.

162 Handsomely decorated antique Chinese porcelain Tray, round form, ornamentation of butterflies, fruits, blossoms, etc., Kea-king period.

163 Very fine Chinese egg-shell Bowl, decoration of flowers in bright enamels, ring and six marks.

164 Choice Chinese *pate tendre* small Plate, very fine blue decoration.

165 Rare Japanese Vase, handsomely crackled, and very fine pink color glaze. Height and diameter 12 x 6 inches ; an exceptional specimen.

16

VALUABLE SPECIMENS FOR THE CABINET.

166 Pair rare camelia green Tear-bottles, old Chinese.
2 pieces

167 Very fine antique porcelain Tear-bottle, decorated in colors, Yung-ching period.

168 Small Chinese Vase, rich black glaze, Kang-he period.

169 —— Another, mustard brown glaze.

170 Choice *Bleu de Nankin* small Bowl, landscape decoration.

171 Exceedingly rare and fine old Chinese bronze Vase, early Ming period, has teakwood stand.

172 Fine antique Chinese porcelain Snuff Bottle, carved ornamentation, green glaze.

173 —— Another, finely decorated in delicate colors.

174 —— Another, decorated with insects.

175 —— Another, finely carved and relief ornamentation of boating scene, etc., Ming period.

176 —— Another, mottled glaze lions' heads in relief for handles.

177 Set (3) elegant royal Kaga ceremonial Cups, square form, rich crimson and gold decoration, blue inscription inside. 3 pieces

178 Choice old *Bleu de Nankin* Coupe, Kang-he period.

179 Pair exceedingly fine Chinese porcelain Saki Cups, delicate pink and canary yellow glaze. 2 pieces

180 Splendid antique Chinese turquoise Vase, hexagonal form with handles, choice quality.

181 Antique porcelain Snuff Bottle, blue clouding, with dragon, etc., in *sang de Boeuf*, Kang-he period.

182 Choice old *bleu de Nankin* small Coupe, fine in texture and color, has teakwood stand.

183 Handsome green glass Vase, from the imperial Këen-lung factory, rare and fine' 'pecimen.

184 Pair antique iron Vases, exquisitely inlaid with gold, interesting shape.   2 pieces

185 Handsomely carved red soochow lacquer miniature Screen and Stand, boating scene, birds, flowers, etc. in relief.

186 Rare and exceedingly fine early Satsuma Perfume Box and Cover, delicately crackled and finely decorated in gold, chrysanthemum flower in relief on cover.

187 Small bamboo Vase, finely carved, with text, etc.

188 Very rare bronze Box and Cover, illustrating cloisonne art, the wires being adhered but only partially filled with enamels.

189 Handsome Japanese sealskin Pouch, ornamented with finely wrought gold figure and clasp, has exquisitely carved ivory fan case attached.

————

190 Splendid old Chinese turquoise Vase, fine in form and color, Kang-he period. Height and diameter 10x6 inches.

191 Rare and handsome Japanese crackle Vase, *Jaune Citron* glaze, choice form. Height and diameter 11x4 inches.

192 Beautiful imperial Këen-lung Vase, double gourd shape, apple-green-ground, with enameled decoration of flowers, emblems, etc., in bright colors. Height and diameter, with finely carved teakwood stand, 11x6 inches.

193 Rare old Ming bronze Incense Burner, fine color effects, engraved ornamentation, finely carved teakwood stand and cover.

2

194 Fine old Corean Bowl, remarkably fine raised work decoration of turtle, frog, crabs, etc.

195 Elegant Chinese antique *blanc de chine* fire Bowl, engraved ornamentation beneath glaze, fine teakwood stand and cover, carved agate ornament to cover.

196 Handsome antique Chinese Jar, globular form, rich blue glaze, Kang-he period. Height and diameter 8x8 inches.

197 Exceeding fine old Japanese bronze Vase, relief and handsomely chiseled ornamention. Height and diameter 13x7 inches.

198 Handsome Chinese hawthorne Jar and Cover, choice in color, religious emblems, flowers and ornaments in medallions. Height and diameter 10x9 inches, Kang-he period.

199 Superb lacquered cabinet and stand, exquisitely ornamented with pure gold and inlaid with pearl and ivory, an exceptional specimen of high grade lacquer.

200 Magnificent old Satsuma Incense Burner, globular form on tripod support, Dog-Foo in relief for handle, and on cover, decoration of a thoroughly artistic character, Buddhist ceremonial gatherings, domestic scenes, etc., in precious metal and choice colors. Height and diameter 20 × 18 inches.

Second Day's Sale.

201 Fine Japanese egg-shell Cup, red glaze with figure in reserve.

202 Modern Satsuma Saucer, floral decoration.

203 Old blue and white Cup and Saucer pierced panels.

204 Tokio small Teapots, finely decorated.   2 pieces

205 Small Teapots, assorted.   3 pieces

206 Chinese porcelain Vases, 2 kinds.   2 pieces

207 Fine old *bleu de Nankin* small Plate, choice in texture and color.

208 Choice Imari Bowl, fine decoration in brilliant colors.

209 Pair fine imperial yellow Saucers, princely dragon in green, seal mark.   2 pieces

210 Very fine *bleu de Nankin* Bottle, straight form.

211 Antique Chinese brown crackle small Coupe, decoration in blue.

212 Fine Kaga Bowl, richly decorated inside and out with precious metal and brilliant colors.

213 Pair richly decorated royal Imari Plaques, octagonal forms.   2 pieces

214 Hezin jar shape Vase, floral decoration in bright colors.

215 Set (3) valuable old Chinese Bronzes, Buddha and attendants, teakwood stand with silver text inlaid.

216 Beautiful lacquered Daimio sectional Box, four compartments, fine gold ornamentation.

217 Choice old Satsuma Teapot, exquisite relief ornamentation of butterflies.

218 Handsome Chinese crackle Vase, cylindrical form, three colors of glaze, brilliant decoration of Chinese historical scene. 17 x 8 inches.

219 Rich Kaga Bowl, very fine decoration in gold and crimson, fish swimming, etc.

220 Pair exquisite small Trays, finest quality of lacquer ornamentation, with fish and insects in pure gold. 2 pieces

221 —— Another pair. 2 pieces

222 Same. 3 pieces

223 Korin Yaki Box and Cover, carved in imitation of section of pine tree.

224 Antique Japanese bronze Hanging Vase, basket design, fine in workmanship.

225 Pair finely decorated Japanese celadon Vases.
  2 pieces

226 Elegant yellow Wall Vase, basket design, Ming period.

228 Fine antique Chinese Vase, jar shape, decorated with blossoms in colors on brown ground, rare specimen. Height 14 inches.

229 Exquisitely decorated Satsuma Sweetmeat Box and Cover.

230 Smoker's Cabinet, Japanese lacquer, decorated with gold, fine bronze fittings, antique specimen.

231 Handsome porcelain Hanging Lantern, open-work panels, fine blue decoration.

232 Rare old Rhodian Tankard, Persian decoration in bright colors.

233 Antique Kioto Perfume Jar and Cover, exquisite decoration in embossed gold, etc.

234 Antique Japanese bronze Incense Burner, figure on sacred bull.

235 Handsomely lacquered Segar Cabinet, decorated in gold and pearl.

236 Fine antique Chinese Dish, decorated with imperial dragons in blue and yellow, Yung-ching period.

237 Very rare old Chinese porcelain Vase, decorated with domestic scenes in brown enamel. Height 14 inches.

238 Pair elegant Tokio Mantel Jars and Covers, richly decorated with domestic scenes, etc., in gold and bright colors. Height and diameter 11 x 9 inches.
2 pieces

- 239 Large Box, circular flat form, *Vert de mer* ground, with flowers in colors, Këen-lung period.

240 Antique Chinese Wall Vase, fine splashed glaze, beautiful color and quality, Yung-ching period.

341 Old *Bleu de Nankin* Bowl, decoration of princely dragon.

242 Elegant antique lacquer sectional Box, gold ornamentation and pearl inlaid, 3 compartments.

243 Small square Flower-pot, Ming period, blue ground with white raised ornaments.

244 Unique Cup and Saucer, antique royal Imari, crest decoration, rare and fine specimen.

245 Chinese Pih-tung, raised designs of dogs and trees in colors.

246 Small Beaker, with lion's-head handles, and fine soft color decorations, Kang-he period. Height 4 inches.

247 Handsomely decorated Tokio Bowl.

248 Fine old blue and white Vase, decorated with butterflies and flowers, good quality. Height 8½ inches.

249 Choice Flower-pot, Kang-he period, figures and flowers in bright colors on white ground.

250 Fine black and gold lacquer Cabinet on stand.

251 Pair very fine Kioto porcelain Vases, handsomely decorated with figures, etc., Zogan border. 12x7 inches.

252 Large and fine Japanese red and gold lacquer Fish, used on festive occasions as a fruit tray.

353 Very fine and rare Chinese Vase, celadon ground with landscapes in bright colors, Kang-he period. Height 15 inches.

254 Handsome Bowl, Këen-lung period, green engraved ground with decoration of birds and flowers in colors.

255 Exceedingly fine antique Kioto Bowl, delicately crackled and ornamented with embossed gold.

256 Blue and white Teapot, with top bail and raised ornaments, Kang-he period.

257 Richly decorated Nagasaki egg-shell Plate.

258 Water Jug, curious shape, with *famille verte* decoration, rare, six mark specimen. Height 10½ inches.

259 Pih-tung, lemon yellow ground with flowers in bright colors.

260 Fine Coupe, Këen-lung period, lotus flower in natural colors.

261 Most delicate small Vase, antique Chinese, double gourd shape, with dragons and imperial seal in bright colors. Height 7 inches.

262 Chinese Wall Vase, peach form, decorated in natural colors.

264 Antique Japanese bronze Vase, basket design.

265 Handsomely lacquered Daimio sweetmeat Jar and Cover, ornamentation of insects, vines, fruits, etc., in pure gold.

Pair large and elegantly decorated Kioto porcelain Flower-pots, on tripod supports, artistic painting of birds, etc. Height and diameter 12x12 inches. 2 pieces

Rare antique Chinese splashed Vase, choice colors and quality. Height 12 inches.

Antique Vase, early Ming period, decorated with fine green and red ornaments. Height 11 inches.

Brown Boccaro Teapot, leaf shape.

Chinese religious Ornament, lotus design, handsomely decorated, Këen-lung period.

Very curious Incense Burner, formed of three elephants' heads, trunks forming feet, mustard yellow glaze. Height 8 inches.

Very rare antique Chinese long necked Bottle, light blue crackled ground earthenware specimen of the earliest period. Height 12 inches.

Elegant antique Chinese cloisonne enamel flower Vase, oblong form on feet, fine in color, and in good state of preservation.

Very fine deep Dish, *rouge corail* ground, with gold ornaments, domestic scene in medallions and birds finely painted on white border, Këen-lung period. Diameter 15 inches.

Elegant Cabinet, lacquered in imitation of steel, ornamentation in pure gold and lacquers, has stand.

Pair handsomely decorated Tokio mantel Jars, on tripod support, fine painting of birds, etc. Height and diameter 12x8 inches. 2 pieces

Antique Chinese Dish, oval form, decoration of birds, etc., in colors.

Ancient Japanese iron Tray, boat shape, raised ornamentation.

279 Antique Chinese bronze color Vase, with yellow borders. Height 6½ inches, fine specimen.

281 Handsome black and gold lacquer Tray, round form, red back.

282 Marvelously wrought antique bronze Vase, representing an old jar, with straw covering and tied with cords. Height and diameter 12x10 inches.

283 Fine bottle shape Vase, with green clouded ground, very rare specimen of the Kang-he period. Height 14 inches.

284 Very fine white *pâte tendre* Vase, noble shape, with two handles formed of bats, rare and choice. Height 17 inches.

285 Splendid specimen of Japanese cloisonne art on porcelain, handsome Bowl, rich in design and colors, inside decorated with crimson and gold, a royal specimen.

286 Elegant lacquered cigar and tobacco Cabinet, pure gold ornamentation.

287 Exceedingly rare, *claire de lune* color Vase, Greek shape, very fine Chinese specimen. Height 10 inches.

288 Handsome Kang-he Beaker, fine powdered blue glaze, with sacred inscriptions in gold. Height 9 inches.

289 Fine square porcelain Box, with cover, basket design, coral red borders and landscape in colors on lid, gold seal mark, fine old Chinese specimen.

290 Beautiful *bleu de Nankin* Plate, elegantly decorated with flowers and fruits, hawthorne border. Diameter 9½ inches.

291 Elegant Pih-tung, white ground, with *famille verte* decoration of landscape, etc. Height and diameter 5½x5 inches.

292 Fine green marbled Vase, in imitation of Venetian glass. Height 8 inches. Küen-lung period.

293 Small egg shell Cup and Saucer, decorated with Chinese domestic scenes.

294 Very fine Kaga Saki Cup, decorated inside with figures of the famous poets, on gold ground, exquisite decoration outside.

295 Small Chinese Cup, lotus flower shape, seal mark.

296 Very fine small Vase, double gourd shape tied with ribbon, mustard yellow glaze.

297 Shirato porcelain Elephant, handsomely decorated, rare and fine specimen.

298 Small antique Kioto Saki Bottle, raised work ornamentation of turtle, etc., finely executed.

299 Antique Japanese bronze Vase, finely wrought basket design.

300 Elegant black and gold lacquer Tea Chest, or tobacco cabinet, lined inside with metal box.

RARE CABINET SPECIMENS.

"A" Finely carved ivory netsuke Landscape View.

B —— Another, older, group of Flowers.

C —— Another, Monkey and octopus Fish.

D —— Another, Goat.

E —— Another, Man grooming Horse.

F Carved wood netsuke, historical subject, Equestrian figure, etc.

G —— Another, Mask, lacquered in imitation of metal.

H Exquisitely carved ivory Button, floral and open work design.

I Superb old Satsuma Perfume Jar, exquisitely decorated in gold and fine colors.

J Old and very fine lacquer Perfume Box, ornamentation of Japanese children rolling snowball.

K Exquisitely wrought silver Basket, floral and basket work design.

L Fine Inro, or medicine case, jet black ground, ornamented with gold and pearl, finely carved ivory netsuke.

M Specimen of Rock Crystal, carved in shape of Japanese peach, fine and pure specimen.

N Handsomely wrought silver Pipe, dragon and cloud design.

O —— Another, design of turbulent water.

P —— Another, smaller exquisite design of Flowers, Butterflies, etc., in gold.

Q Exquisitely carved bone Pipe Case, design of chrysanthemum flowers and blossoms.

R Rare and handsome cornelian Coupe, choice in colors and finely carved, has carved teakwood stand.

S Superb silver and iron Vase, handsomely wrought silver and bronze ornamentation, cloisonne enamel medallions.

T Set exquisitely decorated Mandarin Teacups with covers.   4 pieces

U Rare specimen of metal work, superb Vase illustrating the process of cloisonne art.

V Very fine solid color specimen, small Jar, rich rosedon glaze.

W Exceedingly fine old Chinese ivory white small Vase, *pâte tendre*, relief ornamentation of equestrian figures in procession.

X Fine white glass Vase, from the imperial Keen-lung factory.

Y Very small Vase, antique Chinese *foie de veau* glaze, has teakwood stand.

Z Small Vase, antique Chinese, *couleur de Biche* with decoration in *rouge de cuivre*, teakwood stand.

AA Pair fine Pekin enamel small Trays.

2 pieces

BB Little Vase, fine old *bleu de Nankin*, has teakwood stand.

---

301 Extremely fine long neck bottle-shape Vase, rainbow color, rare specimen of Kang-he period. Height 39 inches.

302 Fine white Vase, with engraved designs in pale green beneath the glaze, Kang-he period. Height and diameter 10x5 inches.

303 Handsome square *flambé* Vase, with raised antique characters beneath fine glaze. Height 8 inches.

304 Pair finest black and gold lacquer Fruit Trays, round form, red backs. 2 pieces

305 Pih-tung imitating carved bamboo, with delicate raised ornamentation of divinities and flowers in dark yellow.

306 Handsomely wrought antique Chinese bronze beaker shape Vase, very fine in color and workmanship. Height with teakwood stand 10 inches. Early Ming period.

307 Elegant porcelain Jar and Cover, white ground with delicate floral decoration in mild, soft colors, the handles formed by horses' head, Kang-he period. Height and diameter 14x10½ inches.

308 Valuable old Satsuma Vase, fine in form, and thoroughly artistic decoration in choice colors and precious metal, procession of Buddhist divinities, etc. Height and diameter 22x8 inches.

309 Extremely fine and large Vase, white ground with ornaments in bright colors, a rare and valuable specimen of the Kang-hc period. Height 23 inches.

310 —— Another, equally as fine, square bottle-shape, decorated with Chinese historical scenes in brilliant colors. Height and diameter 23x7½ inches.

311 Rare and valuable large Fountain, with beautiful dark blue and white vermicelli ground ; in medallion is figure of child holding a basin to a Chinese lady in old-fashioned costume ; exceedingly fine specimen of the Yung-ching period. Height and diameter 22x19 inches.

312 Handsomely decorated Tokio Jar and Cover on tripod support. Height and diameter 15x8 inches.

313 Finely wrought antique Japanese bronze Vase and Cover, lotus design.

314 Smoker's handsome Cabinet, with compartments for tobacco and segars, top panel of cloisonne art.

315 Small Cup, shape of a Sai-See or Chinese silver bar, gold glaze.

316 Small square Perfume Box, very delicately decorated, seal mark.

317 Boccaro ware libation Cup, crackle glaze inside ; rare.

318 Celadon crackled Jar, good old quality. Height 5¼ inches.

319 Very fine small Flower-pot, with black engraved border and blue engraving beneath glaze, Ming period.

320 Choice small Vase, decorated with ornaments in dark blue, Kang-he period.

321 Elegant splashed Vase, Këen-lung period, elephant-head handles. Height 13 inches.

322 *Famille verte* Teapot, decorated with animals.

323 Rare and very fine Folding Screen, made of ivory and handsomely carved, figure, etc., in relief and engraved text,

324 Handsomely lacquered Daimio Toilet Bottle.

325 Handsome black and gold lacquer Writing Box, stork and floral ornamentation, exceedingly fine specimen of old lacquer.

326 Pair small Vases, Këen-lung period, green engraved ground, fine floral decoration.   2 pieces

327 Celadon blue Vase, pomegranate ornamentation in relief, fine form. Height and Diameter 10½ x 8½ inches. Rare Chinese specimen.

328 Handsome Tokio Mantel Jar, richly decorated in gold and brilliant colors. Height and diameter 15 x 8 inches.

329 Elegant Imperial Këen-lung glass Bottle, fine blue color, engraved seal mark.

330 Fine antique Vase with sacred inscriptions in *rouge de fer* and blue ornaments, rare specimen of the Kang-he period.

331 Rare Pekin enamel Tête-a-tête Set and Tray, handsome design on green ground, fine quality and scarce.

332 Fine small flat Vase of good old quality, *flambé* glaze.

333 Exceedingly fine biberon shape Vase, long neck, white ground with fantastic animals in dark brown color under the glaze, rare specimen of the Ming period. Height 17 inches.

334 Fine black lacquer Vase Stand, suitable for above.

335 Magnificent turquoise blue Incense Burner and Cover, mushroom in relief on cover, rare specimen of imperial Chinese porcelain. Height 9 inches. (One handle broken but neatly repaired.)

336 Old Chinese crackled Vase, raised seal mark of the Ming period. Height 10 inches.

337 Handsome imperial yellow Vase, engraved and relief ornamention of Dog-Foo, etc., in colors, Ming period. Height 18 inches. Rare and fine.

338 Light blue splashed and crackled Jar, choice specimen. Height 8 inches.

339 Elegant white *pâte tendre* Vase, with ornaments engraved under the glaze, Ming dynasty. Height 13 inches.

340 Very fine old *Bleu de Nankin* Beaker, Kang-he period. Height 17½ inches.

341 Very curious Vase, representing a cabbage plant, Kang-he period. Height 12 inches.

342 Handsome tea color Vase, hexagonal form, fine glaze, has porcelain stand in blue imitation of rocks. Height 14 inches.

343 Pair elegantly decorated Tokio porcelain Mantel Jars with covers, ornamentation of lotus leaves, birds, flowers, etc., gilt feet and handles. Height and diameter 13 x 8 inches.   2 pieces

344 Beautiful antique Chinese Vase, *lapis lazuli* glaze. Height 11 inches.

345 Very fine beaker shape Vase, Kang-he period, handsomely decorated *famille verte*. Height and diameter 17x8½ inches.

346 Fine small Vase, cylindrical form, rich black glaze with gold ornaments. Height 9½ inches.

347 Large and marvelously wrought antique bronze Incense Burner, representing turbulent water, cover surmounted by figure of Japanese thunder imp. 25x18x13 inches.

348 Magnificent Writing Case, finest quality of old lacquer with ornamentation in pure gold and silver, furnished with ink-stand and water-bottle.

349 Rare Vase, lemon yellow ground, with floral decoration in fine blue, Kang-he period. Height and diameter 11½x8 inches.

350 Ancient Ming bronze Pastel Burner, showing very curious effects of use and age, has finely carved teakwood stand.

352 Extremely rare Vase, square shape with relief ornamentation of figures, etc., Yung-ching period. Height 16½ inches.

353 Superb Bowl, Yung-ching period, exquisite decoration of flowers and butterflies in choice colors, apple green glaze inside.

354 Another, companion to above.

355 Rare cylindrical Vase, fine black ground with ornaments in gold. Height and diameter 17½x8 ins.

356 Pair handsome Chinese porcelain Bowls, decoration of dragons, etc., in fine colors, metalic lustre, Taou-Kwang period.   2 pieces

357 Very fine small Bowl, Këen-lung period, engraved white ground with floral decoration, green glaze inside.

358 Very fine Vase of the *famille rose*, exquisitely decorated with scroll ornaments, landscapes, and flowers, in white medallions. Height and diameter, 14½x8 inches.

359 Handsomely wrought antique bronze Teapot, Persian form, fine old Chinese specimen.

360 Finely carved teakwood ornament Stand, oblong form.

361 Exqisite cylindrical Vase, *famille verte*, decorated with landscapes and inscriptions, Kang-he peroid. Height and diameter 17 x 7½ inches.

362 Rare and exceedingly fine old Chinese egg-shell Plate, pure white paste and glaze.

363 Pair handsomely decorated Saucers, dragons, clouds, et., in brilliant colors, Taou-Kwang period.

2 pieces

364 Very curious Vase, white ground with ornaments, *pâte sur pâte* borders. Height and diameter 13½ x 10 inches.

365 Beautiful lacquered Screen, ornamented in relief with exquisitely wrought silver, gold, bronze, ivory, pearl, and tortoise shell.

366 Artistically carved Kiyaki wood Daimio Box, handsomely lacquered inside.

367 Very fine Vase, white ground with elegant decorations in bright colors *famille rose*. Height and diameter 16 x 9 inches.

368 Handsome Mandarin small Bowl, very fine decoration, children playing.

369 —— Another, decoration of flowers and butterfles.

370 Beautiful chocolate color Vase, two large landscape medallions on white ground, and gold ornamentation on body, fine specimen of Këen-lung period. Height and diameter 15 x 9 inches.

371 Elegant royal Kaga Bowl, square form, gold decoration on crimson ground, rich blue inside.

372 Exceedingly fine Chinese bronze Incense Burner, very rich in color, has teakwood stand and cover, a rare specimen.

373 White Vase with decoration in *bleu* and *rouge de cuivre*, engraved ornaments, fine specimen of Kang-he period. Height and diameter 12½ x 8½ inches.

374 Rare and exceedingly fine Bowl, green metalic lustre with engraved ornamentation beneath glaze, Kang-he period.

375 Handsome Bowl, Taou-Kwang period, very fine decoration of dragons, clouds, etc., in choice colors.

376 MAGNIFICENT SATSUMA VASE, most artistic decoration of Buddhist ceremonial scenes, etc., in handsomely blended colors and gold. Height and diameter 19½ x 10 inches. An exceptional specimen.

377 Fine small Bowl, Yung-ching period, fine decoration of imperial dragons, etc., in fine colors.

378 —— Another, same period, landscape decoration.

379 Fine Antique gold bronze small Vase, Ming period, has teakwood stand, rare and valuable specimen.

380 Rare old Chinese bronze Incense Burner, of the earliest Ming period, engraved and raised ornamentation, showing peculiar and fine effects of age, sold with silk wraps and lacquered case.

381 Curious Corean Jar, engraved and relief ornamentation.

382 Choice tea color Vase, bottle shape, with scroll handles, fine teakwood stand, Kang-he period.

383 Very fine Satsuma Plate, handsome decoration of winter landscape in center, exquisitely painted border.

384 Rare old *bleu de Nankin* Incense Burner, figure of Mandarin lady carrying teapot.

3

385 Exquisitely decorated royal Kutani Vase, double gourd shape, figures. etc., in medallions, richly combined colors, relieved by gold. Height and diameter 15 x 8 inches.

386 Handsomely decorated royal Imari Tray, unusual shape.

387 Very fine old *bleu de Nankin* covered Box, top decorated with Chinese court scene, six marks.

388 Fine Kishiu Jar, melon shape, rich purple glaze.

389 Japanese pottery Saki Bottle, temple drum shape, fine sage green splash glaze.

390 Handsome old Chinese Plaque, octagonal form, very fine decoration of landscape view, figures, etc., in center floral border in choice colors on yellow ground. Diameter 14 inches.

391 Elegant antique Chinese Vase, ovoid form, very fine *soufflet* glaze, *lapis lazuli*, engraved seal mark, rare and fine.

392 Magnificent royal Kaga Bowl, rich decoration in gold on deep crimson glaze, blue dragon inside.

393 Royal Imari porcelain fan shape Tray, handsomely decorated in bright colors.

394 Rare and exceedingly fine Vase, old Chinese, square beaker form, with raised band in center, *gris perle* glaze, height, with teakwood stand.

395 Superb old Satsuma small Vase, exquisitely decorated with fine colors on gold ground.

396 Richly decorated Imari porcelain Saki Bottle.

397 Handsomely decorated large porcelain Box and Cover, early Ming period.

398 Large and handsome old *Bleu de Nankin* Jar and Cover, decorated with Chinese festive scenes in deep blue beneath glaze, ring and leaf mark. Height and diameter 18 x 10 inches.

399 MAGNIFICENT SATSUMA KORA, globular form on
solid base, figure of priest in relief on cover, decoration of a most superb character in delicately
blended colors and gold, figure of Japanese children playing, birds, flowers and blossoms in
medallions. Height and diameter 17x11 inches.
An exceptional specimen of modern art.

400 PAIR ELEGANT SATSUMA VASES, unusual shape,
superb decoration to match above Kora. Height
and diameter 16x7½ inches. 2 pieces

401 PAIR LARGE AND VERY ELEGANT NA-
GASAKI VASES, artistic decoration, figures on
rich imperial yellow glaze, richly combined colors
in borders. Height 36 inches. 2 pieces

Third Day's Sale.

402 Rare Kanzan Saucer, richly decorated with God of Plenty, etc., imperial seal.
403 Exquisitely decorated Chinese porcelain wall Vase.
404 Japanese copper Bowl, curious enameled and painted decoration.
405 Rare Banko-white Dish, octagonal form, finely carved and relief ornamentation.
406 Korin-yaki sweetmeat Box, heart shape, made in imitation of wood, fine relief ornamentation.
407 Richly decorated royal Imari porcelain Bowl and Cover, blue decoration inside.
408 Antique Japanese bronze Incense Burner, group of quail.
409 Very fine Kaga, goblet shape Vase, handsomely decorated in crimson, gold and black figures of Japanese famous poets inside.
410 Choice old Imari Perfume Burner, decorated in crimson and gold.
411 Old Japanese pottery minature Screen, decoration in India ink.
412 Superb royal Kaga Diamio Toilet Box, ornamented and lined with pure gold, crimson glaze, has network covering.
413 Hizen porcelain round Tray, decoration of pomegranate fruit, etc., in bright colors.
414 Ancient Chinese Carving in soapstone, male figure.
415 Kutani Vase, hexagonal form, fine decoration in gold and colors.

416 Fine old Chinese six mark Bowl, handsome decoration of figures, etc., in brilliant colors over and beneath glaze.

417 Very fine old *bleu de Nankin* Perfume Jar and Cover, decoration of boating scene, inscriptions, *₽ /5* etc., has teakwood stand.

418 Handsome royal Imari porcelain Tray, boat shape, rich decoration in blue, crimson and gold.

419 Shirato porcelain Figure, Japanese female artist, robe decorated and glazed, hands and face unglazed.

420 Leaf-shape Tray, rich splash glaze with metalic lustre.

421 Choice *bleu de Nankin* Bottle, crackle and decoration beneath glaze.

422 Handsomely decorated Imari Bowl, fine specimen from royal factory.

423 Ancient Chinese celadon hanging Lantern, relief and engraved ornamentation.

424 Tray made from root of a Tree, ornamented with gold lacquer, and in relief.

425 Antique Bizen Figure, Daimio singing.

426 Fine Kishiu Jar, melon-shape, raised ornaments, rich deep purple glaze, engraved seal mark.

427 Rare and fine Chinese celadon small Vase, shape of two chickens, the heads forming handles, engraved beneath glaze.

428 Handsomely decorated royal Imari Dish, chrysanthemum form, Mikado's crests in relief.

429 Elegant Kaga bronze small Vase, beautiful relief, and inlaid ornamentation in gold and silver, design of maple leaves, etc.

430 Rare antique Cochin Chinese Jar and Cover, engraved and relief ornamentation, rich green splash glaze.

431 Handsome Shirato porcelain Tray, circular form with openwork edge, very fine decoration of flowers and grasses, on basket design ground.

432 Superb lacquer Card Box, with four smaller boxes inside, all exquisitely ornamented in relief with pure gold and pearl, fine quality of modern lacquer.

433 Antique Japanese pottery Incense Burner, globular form, supported by figures of Japanese children.

434 Fine old black lacquer Writing Case, ornamented in relief, with Soochow lacquer, pearl carved soapstone vase, etc.

435 Very fine Japanese bronze Vase, showing rich effects of intermingling of lacquer with the molten bronze, relief ornamentation of pomegranate, fruit, etc., engraved seal of artist.

436 Antique Imari Saki Bottle, handsomely decorated with fine colors and gold, chrysanthemum flowers, figures, etc., in medallions.

437 Exceedingly fine old Chinese blue and white bottle-shape Vase, decoration of equestrian figures, vines, flowers, etc., in choicest blue beneath glaze, has carved teakwood stand.

438 Pair exquisitely decorated Satsuma Vases, ovoid form, boating scene, birds, flowers, figures, etc., in medallions. 2 pieces

439 Superb black and gold lacquer Daimio Bottle, exquisite ornamentation of Tokugawas' crests, etc., in gold.

440 Choice Shirato porcelain sweetmeat Tray, fine decoration in soft violet and bright colors.

441 Richly decorated Imari porcelain Bowl, specimen from royal factory.

442 Daimio Jewel Cabinet, superbly ornamented in gold, lacquer, etc.

443 Elegant old Chinese *pâte tendre* Vase, noble form, rich ivory texture, fine engraved ornamentation beneath glaze. Height and diameter, with handsome teakwood stand, 17x7 inches.

444 Rare antique Chinese Vase, ovoid form, fine *lapis lazuli* glaze, engraved seal mark. Height and diameter 11x8 inches.

445 Handsome antique lacquer Daimio Box, pure gold ornamentation of crests, etc., silver ring handles.

446 Beautiful royal Imari porcelain Bowl, handsome ornamentation of figure of Daimio ladies, flowers, etc., in gold and delicate colors.

447 Rare and fine old Japanese bronze Vase, relief ornamentation of figures, etc., ring handles, engraved seal mark of maker, the celebrated Tou-Won.

448 Very fine antique Chinese fire Bowl, *bleu du ciel la apres la pluie*, elephant heads in relief for handles, engraved seal mark, Kang-he period, has handsomely carved teakwood stand.

449 Antique Chinese jar shape Vase, fine mustard brown glaze, Yung-ching period.

450 Superb lacquer Tray, square form on feet, avanturine ground with relief ornamentation of very lifelike fish, in pure gold, 12x12 inches, an exceptional specimen of high grade lacquer.

451 Handsome Shirato porcelain Vase, with flaring top, fine decoration in rich blue beneath glaze, exquisitely modelled storks in relief for handles. Height and diameter 8x9 inches.

452 Elegant antique Chinese porcelain Bowl, Kang-hc period, beautiful violet glaze inside and out.

453 Rare akai or red pottery Vase, openwork panels, elephant head and ring handles in imperial yellow, metallic lustre and glaze.

454 Beautiful Daimio Box, with cover, circular form, ornamentation of pine tree, lotus flowers, crests, etc., in pure gold and silver, metal bound.

455 Superbly decorated Kaga porcelain bottle shape Vase, ornamentation of flowers, crests, etc., in crimson and gold. Height and diameter 12x6 inches.

456 Exceedingly fine old Satsuma Bowl, handsome decoration of bird of immortality, crests, etc., in green, crimson, and gold, an old and valuable specimen.

457 Splendid antique Chinese Vase, ground tea leaf color, graceful bottle shape with raised rings, an exceptional specimen of the Kang-he period. Height and diameter 16x9 inches.

COLLECTION OF VERY FINE AND VALUABLE JAPANESE LEATHER POUCHES.

Now used in Paris by ladies as chatelaine bags and fan-holders with unique effect.

457 " A." Handsome black pebble leather Pouch, with exquisitely wrought solid silver ornament clasp and chain, finely carved ivory button and leather fan-holder or pipe case.

457 " B." —— Another, finer leather, finely wrought silver and bronze ornament and clasp, handsome silver chain and slide, plain ivory button and leather fan-holder.

457 "C." —— Another, as fine, ornament, clasp, chain and slide of silver, exquisitely wrought, finely carved ivory button and leather fan-holder.

457 "D." —— Another, smaller, finely wrought silver ornament, clasp and slide, bamboo fan case, inlaid with ivory, malachitè, etc.

457 "E." Handsome Pouch, sharkskin, with finely wrought silver and gold ornament and clasp, iron slide exquisitely inlaid with gold and silver, carved ivory button with bronze medallion, and sharkskin fan-holder.

457 "F." —— Another fine black leather, ornament clasp and chain of handsomely wrought bronze, silver and gold, finely carved ivory button and leather fan-holder.

457 "G" —— Another, fine black pebble leather, boldly wrought silver and gold ornament and clasp, agate slide, ivory button, with very fine bronze medallion, leather fan-holder.

457 "H" —— Another, embossed leather, finely wrought silver ornament and slide, bone pipe or fan-case with silver ornamentation.

457 "I" —— Another, very fine black leather, handsomely wrought silver chain ornament and slide, and finely carved ivory button, leather fan-case.

457 "J" —— Another, equally as fine, similar ornamentation with exception button, which has exquisitely wrought silver and bronze medallion—fan-case of leather.

457 "K" —— Another, more elaborate and much finer, exquisitely wrought silver ornament, clasp, slide and chain, and carved ivory button, leather fan-holder.

457 "L" —— Another, smaller, fine black leather with very fine bronze and silver ornament, chain slide and button, leather fan-case.

457 "M" —— Another, larger, boldly wrought silver and gold ornament and clasp, agate slide and finely carved ivory button, leather fan case.

RARE CABINET GEMS.

IVORY CARVINGS, METAL WORK, ETC., ETC.

458 Finely carved ivory Netsuke, Landscape View.

459 —— Another, Chicken Cock, and Temple Drum.

460 —— Another, Japanese Priest and Peach.

461 —— Another, antique, Old Man.

462 —— Another, Group of Shells.

463 —— Another, God of Wisdom.

464 —— Another, Equestrian Figure.

465 —— Another, God of Longevity, and Stork.

466 —— Another, Group of Monkeys, "mother and son."

467 —— Another, sacred Cat, Dove and Rabbit.

468 —— Another, Landscape and Mountain Scenery.

469 —— Another, larger, "Bad Case of Ear Ache."

470 —— Another, Male Figure and Temple Bell.

471 —— Another, Japanese Hercules.

472 —— Another, Boy playing Flute, seated on an Ox.

473 —— Another, Japanese Woman.

474 —— Another, very curious, Stork and Male Figure.

475 —— Another, smaller, The Long-lived Couple.

476 —— Very fine carved ivory group, Japanese God, and Children Playing, has teakwood stand.

477 —— Another, Warrior and Tiger.

43

478 —— Another, Daimio Hunter on Mule.

479 —— Another, historical subject, Warrior, Priest and Deity.

4 —— Another, Warrior and Demon of War.

481 Finely carved figure, Daimio in full Court Costume.

482 Pair carvings in soapstone, Dog-Foo.   2 pieces

483 Pair superb red lacquer Saki Saucers, exquisite ornamentation in pure gold.   2 pieces

484 Daimio Feather Duster, finely carved ivory handle.

485 Small Coupe, old Chinese, engraved ornamentation, fine starch blue glaze, teakwood stand.

486 Handsome pure crystal Ball, two inches in diameter.

487 Pair avanturine lacquer small Trays, gold and silver ornamentation.   2 pieces

488 Splendid silver bronze Vase, exquisitely inlaid with gold, silver gorosa bronze, relief ornamentation in same metal and ivory.

489 Antique Wooden Rice Measure, relief ornamentation in ivory, lacquer, etc.

490 Pure gold lacquer Perfume Box, clam shape, crest decoration.

491 Bone Pipe Case, finely carved ornamentation, lotus design.

492 Exquisite silver Perfume Box, relief ornamentation in gold and silver, handsomely wrought.

493 Rare and fine old Chinese Little Vase, mustard yellow crackle, has fine teakwood stand.

494 Finely modelled Chinese *blanc de chine* ornamental piece, Dog-Foo and Bamboo Tree.

495 Splendid solid silver goblet shape Vase, exquisitely inlaid with enamels, finely engraved and ornamented in relief with gold, gold lined.

496 Handsome antique Chinese celadon Bowl, finely engraved, ornamentation beneath glaze.

497 Exceptional red lacquer large Saki Bowl, ornamented with Japanese treasure boat in heavy gold ; should be closely examined.

498 Very fine old Satsuma Teapot, melon shape, floral and vine decoration in gold, green and crimson.

499 Set Japanese antique Knives, handles of exquisitely wrought silver and gold, all signed by maker ; rare.   4 pieces

500 Solid silver Japanese Pipe, handsomely engraved and inlaid.

501 —— Another, exquisitely inlaid, bamboo branch, birds, etc.

502 —— Another, with ivory centre piece, boldly wrought design, of dragons, clouds, etc,

503 Silver and iron Pipe, bamboo design, exquisitely inlaid with gold.

504 Beautiful old Chinese small Vase, very fine tea-colored glaze, Kang-he period.

505 Exceedingly rare and fine antique Chinese Bowl, showing very peculiar effects of glaze, termed by old Chinese as Color of the Hare's Hair made under the dynasty of the Songs, (960–1279) has lacquer stand.

506 Very fine small Vase, choice quality of old *bleu de Nankin*, exceptional texture and color, has teak-wood stand.

507 Superb silver bronze Incense Burner, graceful form, exquisitely inlaid with gold, silver, and gorosa bronze, figure of Dog-Foo in relief on cover.

508 Exquisite pure gold lacquer Daimio Box, in shape of Japanese ship of treasure. An artistic and high class specimen.

509 Rare and valuable lacquered Screen, ornamented in
relief with curious figures, etc., in carved ivory,
lacquer, etc., finely carved mulberry wood mountings.
—— Another, smaller, similar style of ornamentation.

A careful inspection of the above two screens is
solicited. They are the first of the kind ever
brought to this country.

---

511 Large and elegant royal Imari Bowl, with cover,
richly decorated in fine brilliant colors, medallions in blue beneath glaze, has fine carved teakwood stand.

512 Unique old Ming Vase, three female figures supporting, ornamentation in relief and finely
painted. Height and diameter 15x6 inches; rare
and valuable specimen.

513 Pair exquisitely decorated modern Satsuma Vases,
ornamented with Japanese domestic scenes, etc.
in choice colors and embossed gold. Height
and diameter 10x6 inches. 2 pieces

514 Elegant ornament Stand, carved out of solid block
of Chinese teakwood, lotus leaf design.

515 Fine old Chinese jar-shape Vase, dark bronze
glaze, with splashes of violet, 8x7 inches.

516 Handsome black and gold lacquer, Daimio sectional Box, crest shape, three compartments.

517 Extraordinary bronze Piece, life-like turtle, valuable antique specimen, by the Great Tou-Won.

518 BEAUTIFUL HAWTHORN JAR, Kang-he
period, ornaments and emblematic designs in
white ground medallions, cover and jar mounted
in finely carved teakwood. Height and diameter
of all 13x8 inches. An exceedingly fine and
valuable specimen.

VALUABLE DAIMIO SWORDS.

519 Long Sword, superior keen blade, jet black lacquer scabbard engraved insects, etc., handsomely wrought bronze guard and mountings, inlaid with precious metals.

520 —— Another, very fine blade, scabbard lacquered in imitation of rosewood, artistically wrought mountings and guard, has small knife in scabbard.

521 —— Another, smaller, superior blade, scabbard lacquered in imitation of steel, exquisitely wrought mountings, and guard inlaid with gold, handle of small knife of similar workmanship.

522 Splendid short Sword, exceedingly fine blade, jet black scabbard, ornamented with gold lacquer, mountings of handsomely wrought silver, has small knife and silver chop-sticks.

523 —— Another, fine black lacquer scabbard, superior blade, and exquisitely wrought solid silver mountings and ornaments, inlaid with gold, has silver chop-sticks and small knife.

524 —— Another, equally as fine, mountings of solid silver artistically wrought, has small knife, handle of which is exquisitely wrought and inlaid with gold.

525 Daimio lady's Sword, fine blade, black lacquer scabbard and handle, ornamented with gold crests, solid silver mountings.

526 MAGNIFICENT ANTIQUE CHINESE VASE, biberon form *sang de bœuf* glaze, with rich shadings of purple, Kang-he period, mounted on European brass stand. Height and diameter 18x10 inches. A highly valuable specimen.

527 Superb Daimio Box, with tray inside, most exquisite and artistic ornamentation of landscape
scenery, etc., in pure gold, 7x8x3 inches. An
unusually fine specimen of high class lacquer.

528 Handsome old Ming porcelain Jar and Cover, exceedingly fine decoration of imperial dragons,
flowers, etc.

529 BEAUTIFUL AND HIGHLY VALUABLE
ANTIQUE CHINESE VASE, graceful
shape with raised bands, rich and very even
Blue de Roi glaze, goat-heads in relief for
handles, an exceptional specimen of the
Kang-he period. Height and diameter, with
handsomely carved teakwood stand, 16x10
inches.

530 Magnificent black and gold lacquer Diamio Trunk,
gold plated mountings finely engraved.

531 Finely wrought antique bronze hanging Vase, handsome basket design, very old and fine specimen.

532 Rare Korin Yaki Box and Cover, representing
dried melon, toad in relief.

534 Rare and curious Chinese Earthenware, group
priest, and temple bell, has teakwood stand.

535 Exquisitely decorated awata ware sweetmeat Jar,
gathering of Buddhist priests, etc., finely painted
in choice colors relieved by gold.

536 Pair handsome Vases, Yedo Zogan bronze, black
ground with ornamentation of birds, autumn
foliage, etc. Height 9½ inches.   2 pieces

537 Old Japanese Drum, used by street musicians.

538 Fine Chinese modern Vase, bottle-shape, curious
and pretty effect of splash glaze.

539 Ancient Corean Dish, circular form, carved ornamentation, sleeping figure, pine tree, etc. Diameter 10 inches.

48

540 Elegant mustard crackle Vase, bottle-shape, modern specimen, but very fine even color, has teakwood stand. Height and diameter 14½x9 inches.

541 PAIR BEAUTIFUL TOKIO ZOGAN BRONZE VASES, made by the celebrated Kiriu, Kosho, Kurisha, Shakudo ground, with relief ornamentation in gold and other metals, birds, flowers, etc., silver handles. Height 15 inches.   2 pieces

542 Large and fine Chinese temple Incense Burner, sacred elephant with pagoda on back, figure in relief, handsomely ornamented and glazed, 25x20 inches.

543 Antique Chinese earthenware Hibachi, handsomely enameled decoration in fine old colors.

544 Handsomely decorated Nankin Vase, biberon form, ornamentation of flying birds, blossoms, etc. Height and diameter 12x9 inches.

545 Pair elegant Kaga bronze Vases, exquisitely inlaid with gold, silver, and other metals, Japanese historical subject. Height 12 inches.   2 pieces

546 Elegant Nagasaki Plaque, very fine decoration of landscape scenery, etc., rich border, diameter 18 inches.

547 Superb Tokio sweetmeat Jar and Cover, square form, ornamentation of blossoms, etc., in choice colors.

548 Splendid royal Imari Bowl, most exquisite decoration in richly blended colors, raised ornamentation.

549 EXTRAORDINARY OLD BRONZE TEMPLE PIECE, rocky base supporting two vases and incense burner, boldly wrought dragons encircling each vase, the whole mounted on fine bronze stand, 28x20x12 inches, a valuable specimen of the earliest gorosa bronze.

550 Rare and handsome Daimio Stand, best quality black lacquer, artistically engraved ornamentation, 23x25x17 inches.

551 Elegant antique Chinese Cabinet, handsomely carved, has irregular shelves and enclosures, an exceptional specimen, and rare.

552 Magnificent Daimio antique Screen, chrysanthemum flowers in white and relief on pure gold ground, 6 folds, high form.

553 Rare Chinese ivory white Vase, biberon form with dragon in relief encircling neck. Height and· diameter 14x8 inches.

554 Pair elegant Japanese cloisonne Vases, floral and crest design in bright colors on jet black ground, fine quality. Height and diameter 14x6 inches.
2 pieces

555 Very fine old Kioto Bronze, representing trunk of pine-tree with serpent encircling, insects in relief in gold and silver, all handsomely wrought.

556 Pair handsome *bleu dc Nankin* mantel Jars and Covers, rich dark blue beneath glaze, lizards in relief. Height and diameter 19x10 inches.
2 pieces

557 Beautiful Chinese long neck Bottle, rich splash glaze, with delicate crackle beneath. Height and diameter 21x9 inches.

558 Splendid exhibition Cup and Saucer, exquisitely decorated with lotus flowers, flying stork, etc., on canary yellow glaze.

559 Handsomely wrought bronze Vase, fine basket work design, made in Tokio. Height 16 inches.

560 Rare and exceedingly fine Chinese porcelain Vase, rich garnet splash glaze, *peau d' orange*, Kang-he period. Height and diameter 23x10 inches.

4

561 Curious antique Chinese Vase, boldly engraved ornamentation of horses, water, etc., various colors of glaze, seal mark. Height and diameter 21x11 inches.

562 Pair handsomely carved teakwood Vases with Covers, figures, bamboo and pine trees in bold relief. Height and diameter 13x8 inches. 2 pieces

563 Valuable bronze, large temple Gong, bowl form, made of exceedingly fine metal, and has clear, musical tone. Height and diameter 13x16 inches.

564 Richly decorated Nagasaki porcelain Plaque, ornamentation of peonies chrysanthemum, flying birds, etc., on chocolate ground. Diameter 18 inches.

565 ELEGANT GOROSA BRONZE ORNAMENTAL PIECE, Vase formed by trunk of tree, figure of Japanese children playing surrounding. Height 16 inches.
A very fine specimen from the Tokio Exposition.

566 Handsome Chinese white crackle Umbrella Jar, very fine decoration in choice blue equestrian figures, etc. Height and diameter 25x10 inches.

567 Very elegant Chinese Vase, large biberon form, artistic decoration of imperial dragons, clouds, etc., in brilliant colors on rich green ground. Height and diameter 20x16 inches.

568 Valuable cabinet specimen, large Ostrich Egg, exquisitely ornamented with gold lacquer and in relief, has finely wrought bronze stand formed of three storks. Height and diameter of all 12x5 inches.

569 Superb Japanese silver Cigarette Case, exquisite wrought gold and silver ornamentation, gold lined, Mokumé work.

570 —— Another, similar.

571 Large exhibition Tobacco Pouch, with pipe case and netsuke, bronze mountings, and gilt decoration.

572 Exquisitely decorated modern Satsuma sweetmeat Jar and Cover, embossed ornamentation of birds, flowers, blossoms, etc., in gold and delicate colors.

573 Pair splendid cloisonne enamel Vases, fine shape, jet black ground, with birds, flowers, crests, etc., in choice and rare colors. Height and diameter 10x5 inches. 2 pieces

574 Fine Chinese Vase, bottle shape, with long neck, rich splash glaze of even quality, delicate crackle beneath. Height 21 inches.

575 VERY ELEGANT MODERN SATSUMA JAR and Cover, basket work design, with floral medallions, real "Kakimoto" make and decoration, ornamentation of peonies, chrysanthemums, etc., in red, green, yellow and gold. Height and Diameter 17x11 inches.

576 PAIR SUPERB VASES, same ware and make, shape of Japanese treasure bag, cords and tassels forming handles, exceedingly fine decoration of peonie in red, green, yellow and gold. Height 15 inches. 2 pieces

577 Fine old square Stand, Kiyaki wood, with handsome cloisonne top.

578 Pair lacquered Stands. 2 pieces

579 Elegant Chinese violet Vase, Kang-hie period, very fine in form and color. Height and diameter 13x8 inches.

580 Very fine Chinese modern Vase, biberon form, handsomely decorated in bright colors, Chinese festive scene. Height and diameter 16x11 inches.

581 PAIR ELEGANT JAPANESE CLOISONNE
ENAMEL VASES, design of birds and flowers
in bright colors on jet black ground, fine in form
and workmanship. Height 17 inches. 2 pieces

582 Fine old Corean Vase, handsome enameled decoration in choice old colors. Height and diameter
14x8 inches.

583 MAGNIFICENT CLOISONNE ENAMEL
SWEETMEAT JAR, most superb mosaic and
medallion designs in rich and rare colors of enamels, silver, gold, and brass wires, gold plated
mountings. Height and diameter 8x6 inches.
Prize specimen from the Tokio Exhibition, 1881.

584 SUPERB SILVER DAIMIO BOX, most exquisite and artistically wrought relief ornamentation,
in gold, silver, and bronze design, of peacock,
flowers, blossoms, etc., an exceptional specimen
from Tokio Exhibition.

585 EXTAORDINARY IVORY TUSK, marvelously carved in high relief, Buddhist ceremonial
scene, etc. ; has elegantly ornamented teakwood
cabinet stand. Height and diameter of all
28x15 inches.

586 Pair elegant Chinese porcelain Vases, finely decorated in blue and *rouge de cuire*, Chinese children
at play, etc. Height and diameter 24x11 inches.
2 pieces

587 Finely wrought antique gorosa bronze, Japanese
Fisherman.

588 Splendid Ohto Incense Burner, in form of Japanese treasure sack, supported by three figures of
Japanese children, gilt rabbits in relief for
handles and Dog-Foo in relief on cover, handsomely painted decoration. Height and diameter 13x12 inches.

589 Pair richly decorated Kaga Vases with Stand, relief ornamentation. Height and diameter 15x10 inches.

590 Rare and fine mustard crackle Jar, handsomely enameled decoration of ornaments, emblematic designs, etc. Height and diameter 11x9 inches.

591 Pair elegant Tokio bronze Vases, Shakudu ground, with ornamentation of poppies in white and red. Height 12 inches. 2 pieces

592 Large and handsome Chinese blue and white bottle shape Vase, decorated with Chinese domestic scenes, etc., in choice blue beneath glaze. Height and diameter 21x16 inches.

593 Rare and very fine antique Chinese bronze Vase, raised ornamentation of butterflies, seals, etc. Height and diameter, 23x15 inches. Valuable specimen.

594 Pair handsome *bleu de Nankin* Vases, square form, choice in color. Height and diameter 23x9 inches. 2 pieces

595 EXTRAORDINARY ANTIQUE BRONZE VASE, representing the sea and sea dragon, all in bold relief; exceedingly fine specimen of wax modelling, was cast in solid mould without chiseling. Height and diameter 25x17 inches.

596 LARGE AND ELEGANT IMPERIAL KEEN-LUNG VASE, ornamentation in brilliant colors of Chinese domestic ceremonial and historical scenes in medallion, flowers, text, etc., on light green ground. Height and diameter 36x16 inches.

597 PAIR VERY ELEGANT LARGE VASES, highest grade of Chinese manufacture, unusually fine decoration of flowers, vines, dragons, etc., in white, black and gold on *verte pistache* ground, gilt lizard and Dogs-Foo in relief. Height and diameter, with teakwood stand 41x17 inches.
2 pieces

598 Magnificent carved teakwood Screen, beautifully embroidered black satin center, outside measurement 48x72 inches.

599 Elegantly carved teakwood Bric-a-Brac Cabinet, irregular shape shelves, 63x40x15 inches.

600 Pair handsome carved teakwood square Tables, with shelves and India marble tops inlaid.   2 pieces

600 "A" Pair finely carved teakwood Hall Seats or · Stools, India marble seats.   2 pieces

600 "B" Pair handsome carved teakwood Hall Chairs, India marble inlaid.   2 pieces

RICH STUFFS.

CHINESE, JAPANESE AND TURKISH.

601 Handsome square Hanging or presentation cloth, white brocade silk with satin lining, dragon and crest design.

602 —— Another, drab brocade silk, crest design, crimson crépe lining.

603 —— Another, heavy woven silk, dragon crest in bright colors.

604 —— Another, finer, deity crests, etc., woven in gold and colors, white silk lining.

605 —— Another, fine brocade silk, floral designs on cream white ground.

606 —— Another, crest designs, on imperial yellow ground.

607 —— Woven cloth, crayfish in silks.

608 —— Another, rich brocade satin, floral and vine design on drab ground.

609 —— Another, woven silk crest, and other designs in gold, crimson crépe lining.

610 Handsome Japanese antique silk Scarf, fine colors.

611 Chinese crimson cloth Lambrequin, finely embroidered in gold and colors.

612 —— Another, similar.

613 Piece elegant silk Stuff (Japanese court robe), dragon crests, clouds, etc., in fine colors and gold, on dark blue ground.

614 —— Another, crest designs on black ground.

615 —— Another, crests and arabesques on white ground.

616 —— Another, vine and floral design on light brown ground.

617 Elegant large hanging, woven Silk, design of Japanese deity, storks, birds, flowers, etc., in bright colors and gold on brown ground, lined with white satin. 80x48 inches.

618 Rich Mandarin Court Robe, fine plum color, brocade silk, handsomely trimmed.

619 —— Another, elegant imperial blue satin damask beautifully trimmed and embroidered.

620 Chinese Court Skirt, green silk, richly embroidered and trimmed.

621 Piece elegant Stuff, Japanese brocade satin, vine and floral design in pink and gold on light green ground, about five yards long, thirty-two inches wide.

622 —— Another piece, Japanese brocade silk, birds, flowers, etc., on drab ground.

623 —— Another, heavy brocade silk tapestry, rich violet color.

624 Handsome Japanese silk Court Robe, crest designs on light blue ground, crimson silk lining.

625 —— Another, finer, birds, flowers, etc., on drab ground, cherry crépe lining.

626 —— Another, fan, floral, and vine designs in bright colors and gold on slate color ground, cherry silk lining.

627 —— Another, birds and flowers, in soft colors on gold ground, crimson crepe lining.

628 Elegant Daimio reversible Cloak, fine in design, colors and texture.

629 Piece of rich Japanese Stuff, fine black satin, with floral design, handsomely embroidered in gold and colors.

630 —— Another piece, olive green satin with blossom, etc., in fine colors.

631 —— Another, smaller, old red brocade silk.

632 Elegant Chinese court Robe, old red silk damask, richly embroidered and trimmed, green silk lining.

633 —— Another, rich purple satin, handsomely trimmed, blue silk lining.

634 Pair blue satin Hangings, embroidered with birds, flowers, etc., in brilliant colors, etc.   2 pieces

635 Pair small satin Embroideries, Japanese.   2 pieces

636 Japanese Screen, center worked in gold and silks, Japanese artist.

637 Rich Mandarin Court Dress, fine deep purple figured silk, handsomely trimmed with needlework.

638 Another, equally as fine, violet silk, beautifully trimmed.

639 Mandarin summer Robe, made of sea grass, fine.

640 Turkish Altar Cloth, finely embroidered in gold and colored silks, both sides alike.

641 Handsomely embroidered Turkish Towel.

642 —— Another.

643 —— Another.
644 —— Another.
645 Turkish Scarf, handsomely embroidered.
646 Elegant Turkish table Drapery, richly embroidered in gold and fine silks.
647 —— Another.
648 —— Another.
649 Large and handsome Chinese Hanging or piano cover, crimson cloth, richly embroidered in brilliant silks and gold, 12x7 feet.
650 Pair elegant antique Chinese Door Curtains, crimson ground, flowers, text, etc., embroidered in colors, velvet bands.
651 Handsome Chinese Hanging, imperial yellow cloth with floral design, embossed in red, bound with satin, and lined. 7.3x4.8.
652 Japanese Wrestler's Apron, crimson crepe, with applique ornamentation, Dogs-Foo, heavy gold fringe.
653 Large Chinese antique Temple Hanging. crimson cloth, handsomely embroidered with brilliant colored silks, dragon, floral and other designs.

VALUABLE KAKEMONOS,

(JAPANESE HANGING SCROLLS),

ALL FINELY PAINTED ON SILK AND HANDSOMELY MOUNTED.

Mostly Antique Examples by Japan's Greatest Artists.

⁎ A number to be sold at the end of each day's sale.*

655 Kakemono Sketch in India Ink, Priest and Text.
656 —— Another, Water Scene, Rocks, Sun, etc.

58

657 —— Another, very fine, Storks, Pine, trees, etc.
658 —— Another, Peonies, etc.
659 —— Another, exceedingly fine, Birds, Cherry-tree in Blossom, etc.
660 —— Another, bold Sketch of Tiger.
661 —— Another, Flower, in bright colors.
662 —— Another, Daimio Male Figure.
663 —— Another, choice, Plum-tree in blossom and Bird of Paradise.
664 —— Another, two Stork and Pine-tree.
665 —— Another, Willow-tree, Flowers and Birds.
666 —— Another, Hawk on Pine-tree Branch.
667 —— Another, Turtle of longevity, upholding the World.
668 —— Another, very fine, Japanese historical subject, Warrior and Princess.
669 —— Another, Hawk.
670 —— Another, Japanese Festive Procession.
671 —— Another, ink sketch, The Philosopher.
672 —— Another, Flowers, Crane, etc.
673 —— Another, very delicately painted, Chrysanthemum Flowers.
674 —— Another, highly illuminated, The Death of Buddha and Japan's Lamentation.
675 —— Another, Diamio Musicians.
676 —— Another, Mountain Scenery, Figures, etc.
677 —— Another, companion scroll to above.
678 —— Another, large and fine, Puppies and Crayfish.
679 —— Another, exceedingly fine, Birds with rich plumage, Pine-tree, Rocks, etc.
680 —— Another, old and fine, Japanese Fisherman.

681 —— Another, Buddha and her Court, painted in brilliant colors on gold ground.

682 —— Another, spirited Boating Scene, etc.

683 —— Another, Mountain Scenery, etc., companion to above.

684 —— Another, Hawk, on Persimmon-tree.

685 —— Another, larger, scenes from Japanese Life.

686 —— Another, Figure of Priest.

687 —— Another, Hawk on Tree-branch.

688 —— Another, exceedingly fine, Flowers, Blossoms, etc.

689 —— Another, Peony and Butterflies.

690 —— Another, very finely painted, "The Thousand Storks."

691 —— Another, companion scroll, "The Thousand Turtles."

692 Pair fine Kakemonos, The Long-lived Couple.
2 pieces

693 Fine Kakemono, Japanese Ceremonial Scene.

694 —— Another, God of Longevity.

695 Pair Kakemonos, finely painted, the Happy Rice Merchant and Companion.

696 Kakemono, Japanese Fable.

697 —— Another, Landscape Scenery.

698 —— Another, finer, Lotus Plant, Swimming Fish, etc.

699 —— Another, Japanese Priest.

700 Pair Kakemonos, India ink Sketches, Deer, Monkey, etc.
2 pieces

701 Fine Kakemono, A Visit to Mount Fusiyama.

702 —— Another, very fine, Daimio Connoisseur Displaying his Treasures to Lady Visitors.

703 —— Another, Gathering by the River-side.
704 —— Another, Badger.
705 —— Another, Japanese Philosopher.
706 —— Another, Japanese Pedlar Playing Flute.

DAVIS & HARVEY,

AUCTIONEERS.

www.ingramcontent.com/pod-product-compliance
Lightning Source LLC
Chambersburg PA
CBHW021633270326
41931CB00008B/1010